I0760657

THE

COMMONPLACE BOOK

OF

COMMONPLACE BOOKS

Commonplace books have a fascinating history. They are essentially personal anthologies, where people collect and record spoken wisdom, quotations, poetry, proverbs, thoughts and other material meaningful to them. These books are as old as written literature itself, with roots stretching back to ancient times.

The earliest versions of commonplace books were personal notes, sometimes kept by Greek and Roman thinkers as a way to remember and reflect on knowledge. They often included excerpts from philosophical texts, pieces of rhetoric, and items of cultural or personal knowledge. Roman Emperor Marcus Aurelius, who died in AD 180, kept a famous personal record in this form.

In medieval Europe, scholars and monks used commonplace books to record biblical passages, theological musings, and significant extracts from classical texts. But it was during the Renaissance that the concept took on a new form. Humanist scholars, particularly in Italy and England, began keeping more structured commonplace books to catalogue and store knowledge.

One of the earliest documented commonplace books from this period belongs to English thinker and writer John Locke, who advocated a systematic approach in his essay A New Method of Making Common-Place Books.

This was published posthumously in 1706. Locke introduced a system of headings and indexing to make retrieval easier, likening such books to a 'chest of drawers' and influencing how they were organised from then on. His methods became popular among scholars, and the approach was even taught in schools.

Later, in newly independent America, Thomas Jefferson kept one, which he used as a repository for his favourite quotes from the Bible and moral philosophy. In twentieth-century England, Virginia Woolf's commonplace book was a vital source for her literary inspiration, filled with the thoughts of other writers and poets that shaped her own voice.

Commonplace books continued to evolve, with notable writers, including Ralph Waldo Emerson, Aldous Huxley and W.H. Auden, treating them almost as artistic works. Each entry reflects not only the authors' influences but also provides a fascinating glimpse into their personal lives and thoughts. Today, some people turn to apps and social media as a way to store the writings, images, and ideas that inspire them.

Whatever their form or purpose, commonplace books enhance our appreciation of the Arts and thus our understanding of the world. In short, they enrich our lives.

C.C.B.

POETRY CHANGES LIVES COMMONPLACE BOOK

2024

DHH Publishing

Richmond Upon Thames

TW10 6JA

United Kingdom

www.poetrychangeslives.com

All rights reserved

© Christopher Burn 2024

Christopher Burn is hereby identified as the author of this work in accordance with section 77 of the Copyright Designs and Patents Act 1988

Cover design by Stanford Burn Ltd

This book is sold subject to the condition that it shall not, by way of trade or otherwise, be lent, resold, hired out or otherwise circulated without the publisher's prior consent in any form of binding or cover other than that in which it is published and without a similar condition including this condition being imposed on the subsequent purchaser.

A CIP record for this book is available from the British Library

ISBN 978-19996691-7-1

The last lined pages in the book have been given numbered lines, so that these can be used to cross-reference to the relevant pages, for easy location of items, if desired.

FOREWORD

A Commonplace Book is very personal, and I would not presume to tell you how to use it. But I will share my own experience, in case it helps anyone wondering how to proceed.

I was given such a book like this when aged fourteen and encouraged to record poems and sayings that I liked. I was fortunate to have several teachers who loved literature of all kinds.

At first, I copied poems that I had studied in my English and Latin classes, perhaps knowing that teacher would be pleased. Later, I became confident in my own judgement and included poems that 'sent a shiver down the spine' as great poetry should.

I also started recording quotes and sayings I really liked, partly because this helped me remember them for inclusion into essays and perhaps, conversation (I had a desire to impress). One such was Gustave Flaubert's famous dictum: 'be regular and orderly in your life so that you may be violent and original in your work'. In fact, I wrote it a second time, some twenty years later.

A lot of the writing in my book still exists in my head but I like the feeling that I have a written record for when my memory gets bad. Writing and then reading through my selections over the years has been a calming and pleasurable occupation - even therapeutic.

I don't include my own writings, apart from a few comments, but there is no reason why you should not do so.

The book I was given all those years ago is now a treasured possession and I think that anyone reading through it would get an idea about the person who wrote all those entries.

I hope this book gives you the same pleasure as I have had. Welcome to the world of Commonplace.

C.C.B.

THE BLANK SHEET (La Feuille Blanche)

In truth, a blank sheet
Declares by the void
That there is nothing as beautiful
As that which does not exist.
On the magic mirror of its white space,
The soul sees before her the place of the miracles
That we would bring to life with signs and lines.
This presence of absence over-excites
And at the same time paralyses the definitive act of the pen.
There is in all beauty a forbiddance to touch,
From which emanates I don't know what of sacred,
That stops the movement and puts the man
On the point of acting in fear of himself.

Paul Valery (1871 - 1945)

Ω

Ω

Ω

Ω

Ω

Ω

Ω

Ω

Ω

Ω

Ω

Ω

Ω

Ω

Ω

Ω

Ω

Ω

Ω

Ω

Ω

Ω

Ω

Ω

Ω

Ω

Ω

Ω

Ω

Ω

91

92

93

94

95

96

97

98

99

100

101

102

103

104

105

106

107

108

109

110

111

112

113

114

115

116

117

118

119

120

121

122

123

124

125

126

127

128

129

130

131

132

133

134

135

136

137

138

139

140

141

142

143

144

145

146

147

148

149

150

The Greatest, the most
Important of the Arts
Is Living.
(Aldous Huxley – 1894-1963)